C000201700

DRE-FACH FELINDRE
AND THE WOOLLEN INDUSTRY

WELSH
CRAFTS

Dre-Fach Felindre and the Woollen Industry

J. Geraint Jenkins

Gwasg Carreg Gwalch

© Text: J. Geraint Jenkins
Revised edition: 2005

Published by Gwasg Carreg Gwalch in 2005.
All rights reserved. No part of this publication
may be reproduced or transmitted, in any form
or by any means, without prior permission.

ISBN: 0-86381-964-8

Published by
Gwasg Carreg Gwalch,
12 Iard yr Orsaf, Llanrwst, Conwy, Cymru (Wales)
LL26 0EH
Tel: 01492 642031   Fax: 01492 641502
e-mail: books@carreg-gwalch.co.uk website: www.carreg-gwalch.co.uk
Printed and published in Wales.

Acknowledgements

Illustrations are by David Coviello, the National Museum and Galleries of Wales,
Museum of Welsh Life, St Fagans and Gwasg Carreg Gwalch.

Contents

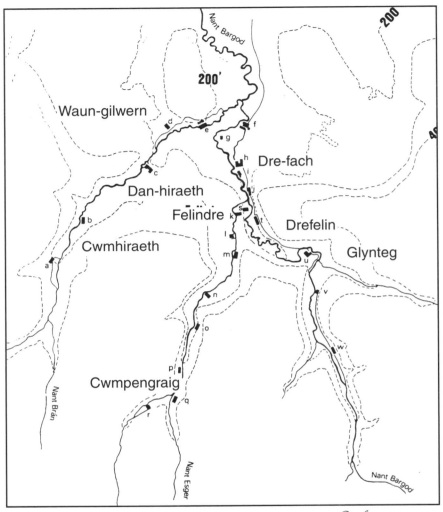

Woollen Mills in Dre-fach Felindre

a	Pantglas	h	Meiros	o	Ogof
b	Frondeg	i	Square Hall	p	Dolwerdd
c	Pant y Barcud	j	Dolwion	q	Coedmor
d	Cawdor Mills	k	Spring Gardens	r	Esger View
e	Cilwendeg	l	Rhydwern	s	Llainffald
f	Cambrian	m	Dyffryn	t	Bargod Mills
g	Pensingrug	n	Dan Gribyn	u	Dôl-goch
				v	Glan Bargod
				w	Cwm Gilfach

Introduction

The village of Dre-fach Felindre is different from others in rural western Wales. It is in the heart of an agricultural area, characterized by dairy farming on the lower land and cattle and sheep rearing on the higher ground. At first glance it is a typical village of rural western Wales, but it is different in that it was until recently the main centre of woollen production in Wales. It was during the second half of the nineteenth century that the character of the middle Teifi valley began to change, for as the woollen industry prospered the domestically based hand-weaving and knitting industry, that had existed for many centuries in the region, was transformed into a factory based undertaking. The population grew rapidly and many migrated from the countryside to the expanding valley villages. Much of the migration was local, but a number of families from the textile producing districts of central Wales did move to Carmarthenshire, especially after 1870. Villages such as Dre-fach Felindre with the associated hamlets of Dre-felin, Cwmpengraig, Waungilwern and Cwmhiraeth and other villages such as Capel Iwan, Pencader, Cynwyl Elfed and Llanpumsaint expanded rapidly. But the most important of all the textile villages was Dre-fach Felindre, which by the end of the nineteenth century had developed to such an extent that a local historian could write: '*Nid oes yn awr o bosibl ddau blwyf yng Nghymru yn troi allan gymaint o wlaneni Cymreig a'r plwyfi hyn. Mae bron holl nerth gallofyddol eu nhentydd a'u hafonydd wedi eu ffrwyno i yrru peiriannau . . . Nid oes braidd ysmotyn ar lan afon ynddynt lle y gellir yn gyfleus i osod ffatri na melin ychwanegol*'. (There are no parishes in Wales possibly, that produce more flannel than the two parishes [Llangeler and Penboyr] . . . Nearly all the power of the streams and rivers has been harnessed to drive machinery. There is hardly a spot on the banks of rivers where it would be convenient to build an additional factory or mill.)[1]

Since the inhabitants of the village of Dre-fach Felindre relied entirely on industry, rather than agriculture, their outlook became much more akin to the inhabitants of the industrial valleys of southern Wales, with whom they had constant trading contacts, than to that of their agricultural neighbours. The villages developed separately from the surrounding countryside and their inhabitants tended to become much more urbanized in their outlook. There was a sharp dichotomy between the villages, which grew so rapidly between 1850 and 1900, and the surrounding agricultural area, both in term of employment and community characteristics. Few of the inhabitants of the village regarded themselves as 'country people', many of their interests were those of the town dweller – the billiard hall, the brass bands, soccer teams and male voice choirs flourished; many families had relatives in the Tumble-Cross Hand district of industrial Carmarthenshire and in the period between the two wars especially, the Labour Party flourished in a district where Liberalism held sway. Undoubtedly, the whole life of a village such as Dre-fach Felindre, was tied up with the processes of textile manufacture and while that industry flourished, so too did a wide range of cultural, social and religious institutions.

Spinning with spindle and whorl, Kazanluk, Bulgaria, 1966.

The Woollen Industry in south-western Wales

Woollen manufacturing was widely practised throughout western Wales in the middle ages and the town of Caerfyrddin (*Carmarthern*) was not only an important wool trading centre, but it also had its guild of weavers and fullers, who wielded a considerable influence on the development of the textile industry in the town and surrounding countryside. That industry was almost exclusively an industry of the scattered homesteads, and although quantities of rough cloth were exported from the port of Caerfyrddin to Bristol and elsewhere, that trade was virtually dead by 1600. The farmsteads of Powys and Gwynedd had become the new centres of the industry and woollen manufacturing in western Wales reverted to being merely a domestic pursuit, contributing to the economic self-sufficiency of the rural neighbourhood. It contributed hardly at all to external trade, but every locality had its contingent of spinners, weavers and stocking knitters who were concerned with supplying a strictly local market. Most of the textile workers practised their trade as a part-time occupation and they carried out their work with the minimum of simple equipment in their cottage and farmhouse homes. A pair of hand cards, a spinning wheel and hand-loom were about all that were required and although in many cases, the textile workers were concerned only with supplying the needs of their own immediate families, some cloth and knitwear was sold at local fairs. Carding and spinning in particular, were until the mid-nineteenth century, very much a part of the daily routine of Carmarthenshire homes and the yarn produced was sold to stocking knitters and a few specialized hand-loom weavers that existed in every district. Cloth could still be taken if necessary, to a fulling mill, for in the records of all parts of south-western Wales there are references to the existence of pandai from the early seventeenth century. Southern Pembrokeshire and the Caerfyrddin district had their fulling mills from the fourteenth century, but they became much more widespread after 1500. The parish of Llangeler, for example, which was destined to become one of the chief textile manufacturing districts in Wales in the nineteenth century had its fulling mill,

Melin Ban y Court, at Pentre-cwrt as early as 1574,[2] but here as elsewhere, textile production was very much a domestic process. In the seventeenth century, specialized domestic weavers proliferated and Dre-fach Felindre is said to have had its first specialized weaver around 1650. He was certain Isaac Griffiths who later moved to the cloth manufacturing district of the west of England.[3] In the eighteenth and early nineteenth century, specialized domestic weavers became far more common and domestic carding and spinning was widely practised. In eighteenth century Dyfed, the textile industry was aimed principally at meeting a local demand. Some cloth was sold at local fairs and those at Meidrim in Carmarthenshire and Capel Cynon in Ceredigion were well-known for the sale of cloth and flannel. 'The wool is manufactured into all forms and colours', said one late eighteenth century observer, 'supplying the inhabitants with every vestment even to his shirt'.[4]

Fulling cloth by treading on it for many hours, Connemara, Ireland.

The growth of Dre-fach Felindre

The second half of the nineteenth century, and especially the last quarter was dominated by the fact that the villages of the middle Teifi valley became the main centres of textile manufacturing in Wales. Dre-fach Felindre in particular became an important textile village and a domestic and factory industry flourished tremendously for nearly half a century. This was a surprising development, for in other parts of Wales, the introduction of power machinery led to the rapid demise of the woollen industry, but here, despite the competition of English wool manufacturers and the distance of the area from the coalfields, there was a spectacular expansion. In 1837, the Royal Commission on Hand-loom Weavers did not consider western Wales worthy of a visit, but by 1900, the Teifi valley was by far the most important textile manufacturing region in the Principality. The development was almost fortuitous for it is virtually impossible to point to any one factor why a remote, rural valley should have become a centre of industrial development.

Undoubtedly, one of the factors that contributed to the development of the woollen industry in Dyfed was the availability of water to drive machinery and to be used in scouring and washing wool fabrics. Many of the mills were built on the south side of the river Teifi, where swiftly flowing streams like the Bargod and Esger fall into the main river to provide a plentiful and constant supply of water. The textile villages too, were in close proximity to the sheep farms of the lower hill slopes of Dyfed, so that there was a plentiful supply of raw material within the region itself. The mills were also within reasonably easy reach of the industrial valleys of southern Wales and when the railway reached Pencader in 1864, and Castell Newydd Emlyn in 1895, it provided the means of taking the products of the industry to its main market in southern Wales. The evidence suggests that before the heyday of the industry there was a great deal of expertise in the region, especially in spinning and the preparation of yarn. At the turn of the nineteenth century, the woollen trade was given considerable encouragement by the Carmarthenshire Agricultural Society, which offered five annual premiums to cottagers, 'who having nothing to depend on but their day labour, who with the assistance of their wives and children living with them, such children not being under 12 years old, shall spin the greatest quantity of yarn from the first day of January to the end of the same year'. Almost every year, the premium was won by someone from the Dre-fach district. In 1801, for example, Jane Williams of Penboyr parish won the first premium for spinning 237 pounds of yarn; the second premium was awarded to Margaret Jones of Llangeler for spinning 198 pounds of yarn; the third was Lettice Thomas of Llangeler for 85 pounds, Jane Rees of Llangeler who spun 75 pounds and the last premium was awarded to Anne Thomas of Penboyr who spun 35 pounds during the year. Domestic stocking knitters and a number of specialized hand-loom weavers who lived in the region utilized the spun yarn produced by the women on their spinning wheels. By the beginning of the nineteenth century therefore, the rural parishes of Llangeler and Penboyr were already gaining some eminence as the centre of a flourishing domestic industry. Cloth

Willowing raw wool in the 'Devil'

Willowing   *Carding engine*

which was woven in the home, could be taken to one of the four local fulling mills. These were at Pentre-cwrt, Dolwion in Dre-fach, Cwmpengraig (later to become Coedmôr Mills) and Y Felin Fach (later to become Square Hall Mills). The last was a corn mill described in an early nineteenth century document as the 'Velin Issa' where fulling stocks had been incorporated in 1776.[5] Dolwion which dates back as a fulling mill to 1651, was developed in the eighteen twenties as a carding, spinning and fulling mill.[6]

A working carding engine scribbler at the National Wool Museum, Drefach Felindre.

Condensing mechanism in a carding engine.

The domestic system

As in Powys in the eighteenth century, carding and spinning on the one hand and weaving on the other tended to be distinct and separate occupations in the Dre-fach of the nineteenth century. Carding, the process of opening up the fibres of wool to produce an uniform web of fibres, was carried out on hand cards, before the widespread adoption of the water-driven carding engine after 1870. There were specialized card-makers in the district; the craft often being associated with that of pin-making. Spinning was undertaken with the so-called 'great wheel', a piece of equipment that could be constructed by any competent country carpenter. Both these essential processes were carried out by women in their homes and it was their work to supply both stocking knitters and hand-loom weavers with yarn. Although for many, carding and spinning were part-time occupations designed to supplement the family income, there were a number of specialized carders and spinners in the locality.

The 1841 census returns noted that there were the following specialized spinners living in the parishes of Llangeler and Penboyr:

Eleanor Eynon (aged 50) of Cerrig-llwydion
Ann Davies (aged 35) of Cwrt village
Mary James (aged 30) of Dre-fach

By 1871 the number of specialized domestic spinners had increased greatly despite the fact that spinning had already become a factory industry, with the establishment of a number of factories. The 1871 census noted that there were 17 specialized yarn makers living in the district. They resided in the following cottages:

Tŷ Sara	Pantyglap	Llandre
2 spinners)	(2 spinners)	(2 spinners)
Penrheol	Pantydelyn	Penbont
Penlôn Newydd	Felindre	Spring Gardens
Cryngae	Wermydd	Penlôn
Bancyrafon	Danyrynn	

Stocking knitting was widely practised in the district, and although many were part-time craftsmen, there were a number of people that specialized in the work.[7] Again, the 1871 census enumerators' returns mention stocking knitters residing in the following houses:

Gellioer	Tŷ Newydd
Dancwarre (2 knitters)	Bronrefel (2 knitters)
Nanteos	Llwyncelyn
Glanrhyd	Wychel
Fedwen	Pantywennol (2 knitters)
Cwmpengraig (4 knitters)	Troedrhiwcryngae
Cnwcybanal	Plygyrhiw
Pit	Brynhorman
Penhiraeth	Ffynnonbedr
Pantgwyn	Nantllan
Ffosywern	Tŷ Newydd
Cwmbargod	Felindre
Penpompren	Pantyfallen (2 knitters)
Penrhiwfawr (3 knitters)	Pantbach
Cerrigllwydion	Blaengilfach
Rhospant	Pantllwyd
Tŷ-cam	Ietwen
Cefn caled (3 knitters)	Llwyncelyn
Pantgwyn (2 knitters)	Soar
Pantydelyn	Penparc
Tŷ Ucha	

Of the 53 stocking knitters, no fewer than 38 were the wives or daughters of agricultural labourers, and it is surprising that no one was a member of the family of a hand-loom weaver. Moreover only one person is described as a 'spinner and stocking knitter', and it is obvious that like the hand-loom weavers, the knitters depended on independent yarn producers for their raw material.

Hand-loom weaving was widespread and was regarded as a distinct and specialized occupation. In 1841, the parishes of Llangeler and Penboyr had 38 specialized weavers residing at

An automatic mule for spinning

Brynamlwg, Pontwelly, Pantydelyn, Pantglas, Cwrt, Troedlôn, Llwyncelyn (2), Ffosddu, Camnant, Drefach (3), Danrallt, Drefelin (4), Penwern Isaf, Blaenwaun, Pantgwyn (2), Felindre (7), Penpant, Panteos, Cwmpengraig, Penbont, Penrhiwledde, Ivy Bush, Dangribyn, Waun, Dan Dinas. By 1871, the number of domestic weavers had increased to 104, and the following were regarded as weaving shops:

Tŷ Canol	Tŷ'r Teiliwr (2 + 1 spinner)
Llainffald (6 weavers)	Glandwr (3)
Tŷ Isaf	Glanrafon (4)
Panteg (2)	Tŷ Newydd
Felindre	Danyrynn
Cefncanol	Spring Gardens (1 + 1 spinner)
Cellan (3)	Blaencoed (2)
Ogof (4)	Clockygroes (2)

Troed-rhiwfach (2)
Glynderi
Pencnwc (2)
Waun (2)
Ffynnonbedr (2)
Ffynnonwen
Berllan
Penlon-Nantlliw
Pensarn (2)
Ffynnonfach
Dangraig (5)
Tŷ-coed (4 + 1 spinner)
Penralltfan
Babell (2)
Penlôn Waun
Penlôn (1 + 1 spinner)
Aberbrân

Top House (2)
Bronhydden
Pantyfyren (2)
Danstar
Dandinas (7)
Penlon-rhadys
Cnwc
Pwllycwm
Troedrhiwcyrff
Quay (2)
Cwmpengraig (3)
Dangraig (7)
Red Lion (2)
Danrhiwcogan
Pantyrodyn
Bancyrafon (2 + 1 spinner)

Some of the mills of the late nineteenth century developed from the weaving shops of an earlier period and there are no examples in the district of a mill developing from a hand spinning establishment. Undoubtedly the hand-loom weavers were considerably more prosperous than the spinners, for a loom together with warping and dyeing equipment demanded some outlay of capital, but the poorest cottagers could afford to buy a pair of hand cards and a spinning wheel. Some of the weavers employed labour and some form of factory system had already entered the weaving side of the industry by the middle of the nineteenth century in the Dre-fach district. Glanyrafon in the centre of Felindre village was worked by four weavers, while nearby Llainffald was occupied by David Jones, a master weaver who employed five others. Some of the master weavers were part-time weavers, part-time farmers. Llwynbedw, for example, was a farm of 60 acres, but three weavers were employed there. Pantybarcud was a farm of 14 acres, but Ben Jones, its occupant from 1860 to 1915, employed four weavers and three girls in 1871.

The Ogof factory in the Esger valley between Felindre and

Cwmpengraig, is typical of the small weaving factories that operated until at least the end of the nineteenth century. The old weaving shop can be seen on the left-hand side of the road, opposite the ruined remains of a later fully comprehensive mill built about 1910.

The weaving shop was a mud-walled thatched cottage on one floor, on the left-hand side of the Felindre-Cwmpengraig road. At the north end of the building was the dyeing room (*y pen ucha*), measuring 10 feet square, which accommodated a pair of vats. Many of the domestic weavers were responsible for dyeing hanks of yarn, and the account book of the workshop shows that red, blue and pink flannel was produced in addition to naturally coloured white, black and grey cloth. In the centre of the cottage was the two-roomed dwelling and on the south side (*y pen isha*) was the weaving shop, 25 feet long and 10 feet wide. This was entered through a door from the tenter field (*y rack*) to the south of the building. In the eighteen seventies and eighties, four hand-looms were operated here.

Some indication of the type of material produced may be obtained from the account of David Jones,[8] a draper from the Swansea valley in 1898. In that year he bought from Ben Jones, Yr Ogof, the following:

	£	s	d
'68 yards 3 + 3 @ 4d. per yard		15	1½
45 yards Brethin stripe @ 5½ d.		14	4½
68 yards Plain grey @ 3½ d.		14	2
68 yards Dau lâs @ 4½ per yard		17	0
68 yards Dau lâs @ 5d. per yard		18	10½
45 yards Brethin plod @ 6d. pwys		16	3
68 yards Fawn @ 3½ d. per yard		14	2
68 yards Plain black @ 3½ per yard		14	2
68 yards Plain grey @ 4½ per yard		16	0½
51 yards Stripe coch @ 3½ per yard		10	7½
45 yards Brethin Stripe 5½ per yard		14	4½
68 yards Pausau x d 7½ per yard		8	4
12 shawls @ 1/6 each		18	0
68 yards Gwlanen wen @ 4½ per yard		17	0'

Ben Jones, Yr Ogof was concerned principally with supplying a local market and a market in the western part of industrial southern Wales. He had customers at Tumble, Cross Hands and Clydach and he attended fairs, usually once a year at Clydach, Llansamlet and Llangyfelach; as well as those held at Castell Newydd Emlyn, Llandysul and other places in rural western Wales. Llangyfelach fair was regarded as particularly important, not only for trading but also as an annual outing. 'Before the railway reached Henllan in 1895, the whole family, father, mother and my brothers and myself,' says Ben Jones' daughter, 'used to travel to Llangyfelach by pony and trap on the Monday morning. We used to stay at an inn at Llangyfelach, setting up our stall in the fair to sell flannel, cloth, yarn and blankets to the miners and tin workers on the Tuesday and Wednesday, then travelled back to Dre-fach on the Thursday'.[9]

Ben Jones was also a small holder and the sale of butter, cheese and eggs was as important as the sale of flannel and cloth. In January and February, 1898, for example, Mr William Evans, Dolwerdd bought of Benjamin Jones, 31 lbs of butter at a price between 9d. and $11\frac{1}{2}$ d. a pound together with:

	£	s	d
'Lining for cloaks $2\frac{1}{2}$ yds.		3	5
5 yds. pink @ 1s per yd.		5	0
4 yds. pink @ 1s per yd.		4	0
$\frac{1}{2}$ dozen stockings		5	3
$12\frac{1}{2}$ yds. navy dresses	1	0	$10\frac{1}{2}$
Cartheny 1		5	0
$7\frac{1}{2}$ yards pink fl. @ 1/-		7	6'

A later account of M William Evans in 1909 again shows the variety of farm produce, and textiles sold from the weaving shop, to a person who acted as a fuller for many local mills. 'The Account of Mr William Evans, Dolwerdd, 1909.'

	£	s	d
'February For dyeing clothes 6-6		6	6
May 9 to 4 yds. shirting @ 1/-		4	0
2 lbs. butter @ 1/1		2	2
October 7½ yds. red		8	1½
Nov. 18 yds. pink @ 1/-		18	0
23 cwts of coal	1	3	0
Dec. Goose 10½ lb. @ 7½ d.		7	5
Eggs		2	6
Eggs			6
Eggs		2	0
April 23½ yds. cersey @ 1/6	1	15	3
May 11 yds. @ 1/6		16	6
July 11 yds.		1	0
August Eggs 1 doz.		1	0
4 yds. shirting		4	0
Nov. 1 8 yds. strawberry		8	8
Duck @ 2s.		2	0
Jan. 5 5 yds. strawberry		5	5
February 11 lbs. lard		4	7
May 4 yds. shirting		4	0
Paid August 1910'			

Ben Jones was an employer of labour, even before he became a full-scale manufacturer of yarn and cloth in a new mill around 1910. In 1905, for example, he employed Margaret Lewis at an annual wage of £13, and a 'skirt dydd Sul, a wythnos o holidays'. The annual holiday was usually arranged at Tumble, a village on the anthracite field of western Sir Gaerfyrddin. Mary Hannah Thomas earned £12 in 1905 together with a Sunday skirt, while the third servant Caroline Williams earned £8. 10d. and a skirt. The fourth Hannah Stephens earned £16 per annum plus a suit of clothes and she was paid as follows:

	£	s	d
'April 19½ yds. black carsey @ 1/8 per yd.	1	12	6
April 28 Cash £1	1	0	0
June 26 Cash £1	1	0	0
Cash 2s.		2	0
Sept. 20 Cash 5s.		5	0
Oct. Cash 2s.		2	0
	4	1	6
	16	0	0
	£11	18	6
Settled Nov. 24th, 1905	£11	18	6'

In 1907 he still employed three – Hannah Stephens 'at £16 per annum and a pair of blankets'; Caroline Williams 'at £12.10 plus a suit of clothes' and a male weaver Johnny Evans, Panteg for £12.10. In 1908 Johnny Evans' wage was increased to £16 per annum, plus a suit of clothes, paid as follows:

'On the account of Johnny Evans, Panteg
Y gyflog am 1908 – £16 a phâr o'r dillad.

	£	s	d
4 yds. black flannel @ 1/2 per yd.		4	8
2 ½ yds. green @ 1/1 per yd.		2	8½
January 12 Cash		2	6
January 24 Cash		4	0
February 19 Cash	2	5	0
Clogs		2	6
March 2 2 ready-made shirts		9	0
May 9 5½ yds. green @ 1/6		8	3
August 4 Shirt @ 4/6		4	6
August 6 Cash	1	0	0
September 22 Cash	2	0	0
October 19 Cash	3	10	0
November One week @ Tumble		6	2
	10	19	3½
	16	0	0
	5	0	8½ '

Warping on wall pegs.

Craftsmen who carried out work at the mill or house were paid in kind as well as cash. In 1908, for example 'David, Carpenter, Cwmpengraig' presented a bill for £4.8.0 for work he had carried out at Ogof. It was paid as follows:

	£	s	d
'Cloth, navy		8	$1\frac{1}{2}$
Cloth		11	3
$2\frac{1}{2}$ yds. Dress @ 1 : 2		3	$2\frac{1}{2}$
October $14\frac{1}{2}$ yds. flannel @ 1/-		4	6
December 1 $\frac{1}{2}$ yd. navy cloth		1	3
4 yds. drawers @ 11d.		3	8
June 14 5 yds. cloth @ 1/8		13	4
June 18 4 yds. navy @ 1/2		5	3
	2	12	$3\frac{1}{2}$
Paid cash	1	15	$8\frac{1}{2}$
Total paid	£4	8	0'

or 'The account of Mr Thomas shoemaker, Newcastle Emlyn.
    20 yards black carsey @ 1/8 per yd.
We had two pairs of boots; a pair of shoes for William 13s. and one
for Martha 8s. 6d.'

In any system of domestic manufacture, an entrepreneur to organize sales and the efficient transfer of yarn from spinner to weaver and the transference of woven cloth from weaver to fuller was essential for the efficient running of a domestic system. The evidence suggests that this type of person was conspicuously absent from Dre-fach Felindre, although some of the fullers were responsible for the sale of flannel. William Evans of Dolwerdd for example, a weaver and flannel dresser took a substantial proportion of the products of the Ogof weaving factory during the last quarter of the nineteenth century. Hannah Davies of Drefelin was described in the 1871 census returns as a 'flannel dealer', and in 1890 John Davies of Aberdauddwr, Cwmpengraig wove on a hand-loom as an outworker for the Coedmôr mills. Most of the weavers were responsible for selling their own produce, mainly to regular customers in the region and the weavers were responsible too, for buying yarn from domestic spinners or spinning mills and for the transfer of cloth to one of the fulling mills.

By 1900, domestic weaving had declined as the industry became concentrated in factories. The decade 1890-1900 in particular was the most important period in factory building and Daniel Jones in 1899 noted the existence of the following factories in the parishes of Llangeler and Penboyr:[10] Babell, Pantglas, Drefach Mills, Meiros, Bargod, Dolwïon (rebuilt 1899); Glanbargod; Cwm Gilfach; Cwm Tŷ Maen; Derw; Henfryn: Alltcafan; Rhydwern; Dyffryn; Dangribyn; Green Meadow (unfinished in 1899); Coedmôr; Dôl-goch; Pantybarcud; Penybont; Frondeg.

Jones noted the existence of weaving factories, excluding domestic weavers, in 1899: – Dôldywyll; Central House; Felinfach; Spring Gardens; Ogof; Cwmpengraig (probably Tŷ Ucha); Tŷ'r Lôn; Gilwen Hill; Parc Cerrig; Pensingrug; Siop Pensarn; Llainffald; Bachygwyddyl; Tŷnewydd; Man-lle-gwaun; Penwalk; Penlôn; Glanrhyd; Nantybargod.

Jones maintained[11] that weaving provided work for about

'260 weavers, and the same number of women and children'. The industry was not without its tribulations. There were disputes regarding the standard price list drawn up by a committee of two masters and two workmen (pp 83-4). There was a strike in 1872 and 1873, and another in 1880 when workmen went on strike for seventeen weeks. There was another in 1891, when there was controversy regarding the payment of weavers according to the length of the warping wall, and another of six months duration in 1894. Following that strike, prices were reduced by 2s. 1d. a £ from that appearing on the list. These price lists give a clear indication of the type of product produced by the industry and the payment of weavers.[12]

Hand-loom weaving

Hand-loom weaving workshops in Dre-fach Felindre 1871-1900

Aberdauddwr (1)
Bryn (2)
Brogynnydd (2)
Castle Green (1)
Central House (1)
Clynderi* (1)
Lôn Fawr (1)
Dandinas* (7)
Danwaring (1)
Danrhiw (1)
Danyrynn (2)
Ffynnonfach (2)
Glandwr* (3)
Gilwen Terrace (1)
Groesffordd (1)
Lôn Fawr (1)
Llainffald* (6)
Nantybargod (1)
Pantmelyn (1)
Penlon Nantlliw* (1)
Pencnwc* (2)
Pwllycwm* (1)
Penlôn Noddfa (1)
Quay* (1)
Red Lion* (2)
Spring Gardens (1)
Troedrhiwfach* (1)
Top House* (2)
Tŷ Nicholas (1)
Tŷ'r Lôn (4)

Babell* (2)
Bancyrafon* (2)
Clunglas (1)
Cefn Canol* (1)
Cilgraig (1)
Cnwc* (1)
Cross Lane* (6)
Nantllin (1)
Dangraig* (5)
Danrhiw Cogan (1)
Tŷ Ucha (2)
Ffynnonbedr (2)
Green Park (1)
Glanrhyd (1)
Yr Hall (1)
Penrhiw fawr isaf(1)
Llwynbedw* (4)
Nantyrefail (1)
Penlôn* (2)
Pantyfyren* (2)
Panteg* (2)
Parcerrig (2)
Pensarn* (1)
Tŷ Bach (Esger Villa) (1)
Rhydhalen (1)
Tŷ Canol* (1)
Tŷ Newydd* (1)
Tŷ Coed* (4)
Tŷ Ricey (1)
Tŷ'r Lôn (3)

Bachygwyddyl (2)
Berllan* (1)
Bronhydden* (1)
Cwm Cottage (1)
Clockygroes* (2)
Collan* (3)
Cwrtnewydd (1)
Dôldywyll (1)
Penpit (1)
Danstar* (1)
Felinfach* (1)
Ffynnonwen* (1)
Glanyrafon* (4)
Glyn (1)
Lôn* (1)
Man-lle-Gwaun
Tŷ Newydd (1)
Ogof (4)
Pantyrodyn* (1)
Penlôn Waun* (1)
Penralltfan* (1)
Penbont (1)
Penwalk (1)
Siop Pensarn* (2)
Troedrhiwcyrff* (1)
Tŷ Isaf* (1)
Tŷ Bwtsiwr (2)
Tŷ'r Iet (1)
Waun* (2)

* *Enumerated in 1871 census. The others worked between 1880 and 1900. Numbers in brackets denote number of weavers employed.*

The growth of the mills

Fully comprehensive mills where all the processes of woollen production were concentrated did not become really common in the Dre-fach Felindre district until after 1880. From then until 1914, mills sprang up at a considerable rate. Of course there were mills for carding, spinning and fulling in the district, well before 1880, but it was only after that date that the movement from homestead to factory gathered pace.

As early as the first decade of the nineteenth century, carding machinery in the form of water-driven scribbler carders was introduced into a mill at Cwmpengraig; into a building that had been in existence for some time as a fulling mill. The mill was later known as Coedmôr and in the eighteen twenties its owner Deio Siah installed a spinning jack of 40 spindles.[13] Coedmôr continued as a carding, spinning and fulling mill until 1878, when it was rebuilt by John Phillips as a fully comprehensive mill. In addition to yarn preparation and cloth finishing, flannel was woven on the premises on 18 hand-looms. Phillips also employed some hand-loom weavers as outworkers and he may be regarded as one of the entrepreneurs of Dre-fach Felindre, responsible not only for processing on his premises, but also for the sale of cloth, the organization of domestic weavers and for finishing woven cloth at a fulling mill.

Dolwion in Dre-fach also began as a fulling mill, and both carding and spinning machinery was introduced into the mills in the eighteen twenties. According to the 1871 census, Dolwion was occupied by John Adams, who also ran a 20 acre farm and employed two women, Elizabeth Davies as a spinner and Ruth Davies as a carder. Adams himself and his daughter Margaret, who in 1893 demonstrated weaving at the Chicago World Fair, were weavers.

Not all the early nineteenth century mills were incorporated in already existing *pandai*. Llwynbedw, later to become Dyffryn Mills, was built especially by John Lewis around 1835 as a carding, spinning and weaving mill. It contained scribbler and condenser carders, a partly water-driven mule of 120 spindles and a number

A power loom – Dobcross

of hand-looms. According to the census of 1871, Samuel Williams, whose family had owned the mills from around 1845, employed 20 men and women and 3 boys. Of these 3 were spinners, 1 was a carder and the remainder were weavers. Samuel Williams was a pioneer of textile manufacturing in the district; for many years was the leading figure on the committee that periodically drew up the price and wages list for weavers; he was one of the first to produce textiles right through from the initial sorting of wool to finishing. His example was soon followed by other mill owners, with the result that the specialized fulling mills closed or ceased to specialize and domestic spinning virtually disappeared. The introduction of spinning machinery brought severe discontent to the hand spinners of Dre-fach Felindre, especially when the first 'jacks' were introduced in the eighteen twenties and thirties. But as more machinery was introduced and as those machines became increasingly larger in size, there was very little that the independent spinner could do except accept the situation. It is significant that in 1871, when the writing was already on the wall for the domestic spinner, that the average age of the women employed in the trade was as high as 64 years of age compared with an average for hand loom weavers of 39 years. In the declining years of hand-spinning, only the elderly still clung to a trade that was being superseded at a rapid rate by more modern power-driven equipment. The hand-loom weavers held on a little longer, although by 1900 most of them were employed as weavers in factories.

During the last quarter of the nineteenth century, the Dre-fach Felindre district entered a period of unprecedented prosperity, a large proportion of the trade being aimed at the mining and metallurgical valleys of southern Wales. Certain mills concentrated on certain areas and mill owners had long standing agreements with drapers in southern Wales industrial towns. For example, Pantybarcud mills sent much of their product to drapers in Maesteg, Aberdare and Port Talbot while flannel from Pantglas mill, Cwmhiraeth was sent to the Sir Fynwy and Rhondda valleys in particular.

With the development of the industry between 1890 and 1914, machinery, often second-hand machinery from Yorkshire mills was purchased by the textile manufacturers. Ben Jones of the Ogof Factory for example, when he decided to convert his weaving shop to a fully comprehensive mill built a new building across the road from the old weaving shop. This was equipped with a 48 inch scribbler and carder to produce 24 good threads, a hand mule of 240 spindles, a 44 inch power loom and three 38 inch power looms. John Jones of Bargod mills equipped his new mill building about 1890 with a 48 inch carding engine producing 20 threads, a hand mule of 200 spindles, two 45 inch and one 40 inch looms.

The arrival of the railway at nearby Henllan in 1895 provided

General view of Dre-fach Felindre

Entrance to Felin Rhydwern, Felindre

Henllan station in its heyday, circa 1910

Henllan station today – a tourist attraction.

Ceramic panel on roadside at Dre-fach Felindre.

Melin Rhydwern in 2004

Disused buildings at Melin Dyffryn

Name plate on wall of disused mill.

Melin Dyffryn

*Mill leat over Nant Esger
at Melin Dyffryn*

Ogof weaving shed with loom house on the left.

Melin Dolwion, built on the site of an early pandy

Melin Dolwerdd

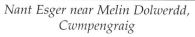

Nant Esger near Melin Dolwerdd,
Cwmpengraig

Melin Dolwerdd

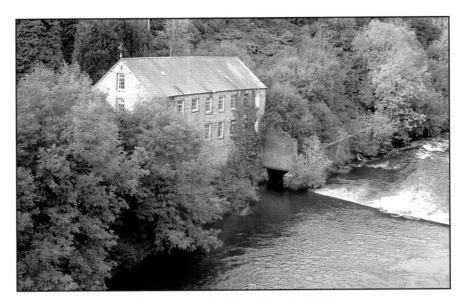

The remains of Melin Alltcafan, 2004.

Melin Alltcafan in 1975

Melin Meiros, now a tent factory

*Gate to Melin Cambrian, now the entrance
to the National Woollen Museum*

Entrance to the National Woollen Museum

Water wheel at the museum

The main weaving shed of Melin Cambrian – now the main museum building

Sied wynt *(wind shed) for drying shawls in an open-sided building*

Llysiau'r cribwr *(teasels) on banks* of Nant Bargod

Museum entrance

Finished products

Power loom – warp roller

Power loom – heddles

Jacquard loom for patterned cloth

43

Nursing shawl in the loom at Melin Teifi

Twister, Melin Teifi

Cone winder

Detail of winder

Warping mill

Raymond Jones of Melin Teifi preparing the warp (ystof) on a power loom

Broad loom for blankets – Dobcross

Narrow loom for cloth and flannel – Hattersley pedal loom

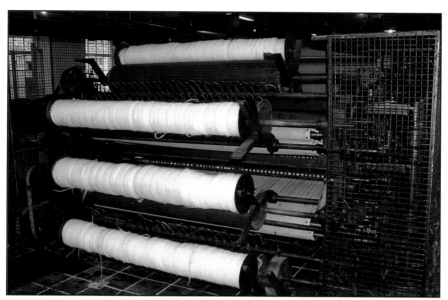

Carded wool ready for spinning on tape condenser

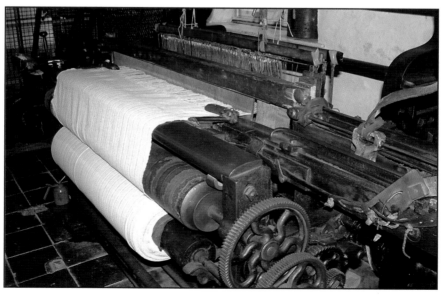

Finished weave on the narrow-width flannel loom: Butterworth & Dickinson

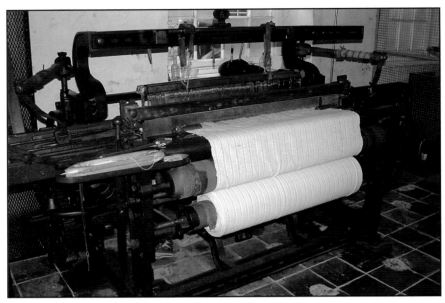

Butterworth & Dickinson power loom

Hot press for blankets and shawls

Teasel gig for napping cloth

the impetus for a rapid development of the industry. The large Alltcafan Mills at Pentre-cwrt, originally called Cafan Bridge Mills were built in close proximity to the railway in the late nineties and smaller factories like Llainffald in Felindre were re-built and enlarged and became something more than mere weaving sheds. Whereas before, these mills were dependent on yarn carded and spun in specialized yarn factories or by domestic spinners, they now installed power machinery to deal with all processes of textile manufacture.

The industry attracted labour from other areas not only to work in the textile industry but also to actually build mill buildings. Many Irish labourers settled in Drefelin for example, to such an extent that a local anonymous poet could write:[14]

> O claddwch y Gwyddelod,
> Naw troedfedd yn y baw,
> Ac arnynt rhowch yn helaeth,
> O ffrwyth y gaib a rhaw,
> A rhoddwch arnynt feini,
> A rheiny o dan sêl,
> Rhag ofn i'r diawled godi
> A phoeni'r oes a ddêl.

By 1900 prosperity reigned in Dre-fach Felindre so that a contemporary observer could write: 'The unhealthy and smoke filled cottages have disappeared and beautiful new houses have been built everywhere. Craftsmen in many trades are more numerous and in constant work; the rateable value of the houses is so great that the burden on farmers has been lightened'.[15]

The mills

Alltcafan
A large mill on the banks of the Teifi, alongside the railway line near the village of Pentre-cwrt. The mill was built in 1895 as the Cafan Bridge Mills by David Rees. Rees was succeeded as owner by Ben Jones, a weaver at Central House in the village of Dre-fach, and then by his son Tom Jones and his daughter and son-in-law, Beryl and William James. In 1972 the mill was purchased by Dafydd Gapper. Since 1970, there had been a sharp decline in the range of products, the processes and the number of people employed at Alltcafan. Closed 1981. Partly demolished in 1996.

Bargod Mills
Established c. 1890 by John Jones, whose son ran it with the assistance of his wife and two men until it closed c. 1950. This is a two storeyed building with a dwelling attached, on the banks of the Bargod near the centre of Dre-fach.

Cambrian Mill
The largest of the Dre-fach mills which started as the weaving shop of the Doldywyll, dating back to about 1840. In 1899, it was occupied by David Davies but between 1910 and 1912, it was rebuilt by David Lewis of Pantglas; it was expanded and re-equipped to become a very large comprehensive mill employing over 50 people. Until 1951, the owner was John Lewis, the son of its founder, but in that year it was purchased by Messrs, David Evans Bevan Ltd., of Neath, the ownership passing over to the Tra-môr Company in 1968. Purchased by the National Museum of Wales 1984. Now in full production with part of the mill leased to D.R.V. Jones. Houses the National Woollen Museum.

Cawdor Mills (Aberbrân)
A weaving shop in the village of Waungilwern converted into a mill on the river Brân by D. H. Lewis. It last worked in the nineteen twenties.

Cilwendeg

Was once one of the largest mills in Dre-fach, and was established about 1880. The last owners were Messrs. D. Williams & Sons, who closed the factory in the late nineteen twenties. Later the Teifi Valley Leisure Centre.

Coedmôr

This was one of the first factories in the district established in the eighteenth century as a fulling mill at Cwmpengraig. It was operated by the son of John 'Twcwr', Pensingrug. It was he who built another fulling mill downstream of Cwmpengraig at Dolwerdd. The first spinning 'jack' of 40 spindles was introduced in the Coedmôr mill in the eighteen twenties. The mill was rebuilt in 1878 for carding, spinning and weaving on hand looms and was occupied by John Phillips. He was succeeded by John Lewis of Aberaeron whose son operated the mill until it closed in the nineteen fifties. The mill was burnt to the ground during the depression of the nineteen twenties; it was rebuilt but it was burnt again about 1950. In 1947 it employed 7 men and 4 girls with 2 occasional female workers.

Cwm Gilfach

Located high up the Bargod valley, beyond Drefelin. It was established in the eighteen eighties for spinning and weaving by John W. Jones. It was closed in 1923 and the building converted into a dwelling house.

Derw Mills

It was the largest of the Welsh mills, located near the village of Pentre-cwrt. Established 1890 by John Jones, whose daughter married Gwilym E. Lewis a brother of John Lewis, Cambrian Mills, Dre-fach. This, the most modern of Welsh mills was run by the Lewis family, until its closure in 1981. It was then operated briefly by Gareth Poulson. The mill is now a fine furniture workshop.

Dangribyn (Glanesger)

A weaving shop employing 4 weavers in 1871. The occupant was also concerned with farming a holding of 9½ acres. In the 1890s Thomas Jones operated the mill until it closed in 1945. It was equipped with carding, spinning, weaving and knitting machinery.

Dôl-goch
A large mill in the centre of Drefelin. It was built about 1890 by Henry Davies who operated it until 1940. It was then taken over by Gustav Brdlik, a Czech refugee who came to Britain in 1911 and was operating the Glanbargod mill. It closed in 1963.

Dolwion
The earliest factory in Dre-fach (established c. 1820). It began as a fulling mill in the eighteenth century with carding and spinning machinery being incorporated in the mill in the 1820s. The owner in 1871 was John Adams but in 1901 it was taken over by David Jones whose family operated the mill until it finally closed in 1972. During its last decade of operation, stocking knitting and the wholesaling of the products of other mills were the only activities carried out at Dolwion.

Dre-fach Mills (see Square Hall)

Dyffryn
An early mill rebuilt in the 1920s. Llwynbedw was one of the first factories in the district and John Lewis was carding, spinning and weaving in the mill in the 1830s. His daughter and son-in-law built Pantybarcud and another daughter with her husband – Mr and Mrs Williams built another mill near Llwynbedw and called it Dyffryn. Its owner in 1871, Samuel Williams, employed 23 people, and he was a pioneer of textile production in the district for he was the first to produce textiles from the preparation of yarn to weaving under the same roof. He erected two water wheels one above the other at the gable end of Dyffryn. The water from the top wheel dropped on to the second wheel, thus producing double power with the same water. He had shops to sell his cloth as far away as Middlesbrough. Samuel Williams was followed as owner by John Davies of Pensarn. Samuel Lewis of Meiros Hall and in

Dolwion today

Melin Dyffryn

1946 by Maldwyn Williams. In 1970 the mill passed on to Frank Davies, producing a variety of flannel, blankets and furnishing fabrics, until its closure in the 1980s.

Esger View (Tŷ Uchaf)
Located in the Esger valley, 200 yards upstream from the hamlet of Cwmpengraig. It originated as a weaving shop owned by James Evans, and in the 1880s it was operated by Daniel and Frances Rees who developed it as a fully comprehensive mill circa 1903. It closed about 1950.

Frondeg
A comprehensive mill near the hamlet of Cwmhiraeth. Its owner from about 1880 until it was burnt in the 1920s was Daniel Lewis who with Samuel Williams, Dyffryn represented the mill owners on the committee that priced Dre-fach textiles.

Glanbargod
Established in the 1890s. Occupied by Gustav Brdlik until his death in a fire at the mill in 1970. Its previous owner was John Jones.

Green meadow (Dolwerdd)
Built in 1899 by David Jones on the site of an earlier fulling mill. Closed in the 1920s, but reopened in 1969 by Arthur Morus as a weaving factory that still operates.

Henfryn
Located on the road to Alltcafan, Pentre-cwrt. Operated from about 1890 to the 1920s by William L. Davies and his son D. A. Davies.

Llainffald
A weaving shop in Felindre employing 5 weavers in 1871, occupied by David Jones. Power looms, a carder and a mule were introduced in the 1890s. The last occupant was Samuel Baker-Jones and the mill was burnt in the nineteen twenties.

Llwynbedw (see also Dyffryn)

This was a weaving factory employing 3 weavers in 1871. The weaver John Lewis ran a 60 acre farm in addition. A mule of 120 spindles was incorporated into the building in the 1860s.

Meiros

A large mill in the centre of Dre-fach. It was built in the 1890s by John Lewis and he was followed as owners by Eiffel Lewis and Bedford. The mill, now a tent making factory, was destroyed by fire in the 1920s; it was rebuilt in red brick, only to close again in 1940.

Melin Dolwerdd, Cwmpengraig

Ogof

A weaving shop between Felindre and Cwmpengraig converted by Ben Jones into a fully comprehensive mill, early in the twentieth century. Burnt in the 1920s.

Pantglas

A fully comprehensive mill at Cwmhiraeth, owned by David Lewis. David Lewis set up the Cambrian Mills and the machinery was moved from Pantglas.

Pantybarcud

A comprehensive mill off the Cwmhiraeth road built by Ben Jones about 1860. In 1871 he ran the mill with the assistance of 4 weavers and 3 girls and farmed 14 acres of land. Ben Jones was followed by John Lewis who in 1915, went to run the Maesllyn mills, Coed-y-bryn. The owner of the mill from 1915 until it closed in 1957 was George Campden.

Pensingrug

Near the centre of Dre-fach. A fulling mill and flannel dressing shop dating back to the 1820s. Kept by John and David Williams who installed looms and later by Samuel and Elizabeth Jones. Samuel Jones left the mill c. 1880 and set up Trebedw Mills, Henllan.

Rhydwern

A mill established at Felindre on the Cwmpengraig road in 1895. Built by John Jenkins, Troedyrhiw. Its first occupant was a weaver, David Davies of Tŷ'r Nyddu, Man-lle-gwaun. He was followed by his son-in-law, David Jones, whose sons occupied the mill until it closed in 1960. Run in conjunction with a smallholding.

Spring Gardens

A hand-loom weaving shop in Felindre. In 1900 power looms installed there by the owner. David Jones, to weave yarn which he prepared at another mill that he owned at Cwm Morgan.

Yr Ogof, an early hand-loom weaving workshop; the dyeing section is to the right.

Square Hall

Probably built on the site of an early fulling mill, described as 'Y Felin Isa' in the centre of Dre-fach village. Hand-loom weaving was carried on there throughout the nineteenth century, but in the 1890s the adjacent corn mill, Y Felin Fach, was converted into a woollen mill by David Evans. The mill closed in the 1950s and the substantial building is now used as a furniture warehouse.

The golden era

For a short time, Dre-fach Felindre enjoyed a golden era as the most important textile manufacturing district in the whole of Wales. It was a short-lived prosperity which did not really begin until the eighteen eighties but was to end shortly after the end of the first world war. During that period of little more than a quarter of a century there was a constant demand for the products of the looms; fortunes were amassed by the owners of the mills who could call on an adequate pool of cheap labour. In the village, children soon followed their parents to work in textile mills, indeed mill-owners expected that the children of their employees should work at the textile factories; and one informant describes how children were expected to join their parents at work in a textile mill, as soon as they were ten years of age. This was during the first decade of the

Dolwion, a mill built on the site of an early pandy.
Operated for many years by the Adams family, one of whom – John Adams –
became the second president of the U.S.A.

last century; the main work of young children being to look after the carding engines. Usually, children of school age worked from five in the evening until eight for which they were paid the princely sum of three pence in 1907. In addition they were expected to work on Saturday morning from 8.00 a.m. until 1.00 p.m. for which they were paid four pence. During the first decade of the twentieth century, there are many tales of victimization when weavers were dismissed from employment for refusing to allow their children to work in mills that were often cold and damp. 'Very few of the children of weavers were given any secondary education,' said one informant. 'One mill-owner, on being told that a certain weaver's child would not be coming to work said, "If your boy doesn't come here to work then there is no room for you. Go and find another job". There was nothing for it then but to go and work in the coalmines of Cross Hands or Tumble for if you upset one mill-owner you'd upset the lot'.

Apprenticeship as a textile worker lasted for three years and it was customary in Dre-fach to have one apprentice to every four experienced workman. During the first year, the apprentice did nothing except look after the carding engines and payment in 1905 was ten pence a day for a six-day week. The working day lasted for twelve hours, the workers starting at either 7 a.m. or 8.00 a.m. Around 1907 when a five and a half day week became the rule, some of the workers were still expected to work in the mill for six full days. Dyeing and washing, where little machinery was required, and there was therefore no noise, were the usual tasks performed on Saturday afternoons. Local women were expected to take shawls and blankets to their homes for fringing and hemming over the week-ends.

During the first decade of the twentieth century, there was considerable discontent in the factories of Teifi-side; the main complaint being that mill-owners were refusing to start payment to their employees until the end of the working week or 1.00 p.m. on Saturday. Payment of wages was often not completed until 3.00 p.m.

Payment to workers was not high. The small mills that employed two or three workers, usually hired them at an annual wage. The Ogof factory for example, between 1911 and 1916 paid:

Getta James	annual wage for 1911	£16.15s.
Mary Jane Evans	annual wage for 1911	£11.10s.
Margaret Ann Jones	annual wage for 1912	£13.00 plus a suit of clothes
Mary Jane Evans	annual wage for 1912	£12.10s.
Mary Jane Evans	annual wage for 1913	£13.00 plus a shirt
Margaret Ann Jones	annual wage for 1913	£13.10s. plus a shirt
Rachel Newman	annual wage for 1913	£11.10s.
Mary Jane Evans	annual wage for 1914	£14.00
Hannah Evans	annual wage for 1914	£14.00 plus 5 yds. of flannel
Hannah Evans	annual wage for 1915	£14.10s plus skirt
Rachel Newman	annual wage for 1916	£12.00 plus suit of clothes
Annie Jones	annual wage for 1916	£16.00
Anne Davies	annual wage for 1916	£15.00

The larger mills employing half a dozen or more workers, had a strict division of labour within them. There were spinners and weavers, carding-engine minders and finishers, shawl makers and shirt makers. A local committee of four that determined the piece-rate wage to be paid to weavers, operated in the district between about 1880 and 1920. The committee consisted of two masters and two workmen and it was their task to specify the piece-rate paid for every type of fabric. According to the 1891 list this varied from $3\frac{1}{2}$ d. per yard for striped flannel to $8\frac{1}{2}$ d. per yard for worsted. A 20 yard length of warp was paid at the rate of 6d. per piece; spinners in 1905 were paid a fixed wage of 18 shillings a week rising to 25 shillings a week after five years service.

In the hey-day of Dre-fach as a centre of manufacture, there were two types of factory. In the first place there were the small mills, employing principally a mill-owner's family and perhaps one or two employees. In many cases the working mill-owner worked the mill in conjunction with a smallholding. Glanesger

Alltcafan Mills, Pentre-cwrt in its heyday.

(Dangribyn) mill, Ogof, Pantybarcud and Rhydwern were examples of this type of mill where the occupant was also concerned with farming.

Some of these rural mills were inaccessible, for they were located near adequate water power supplies rather than within reach of easy marketing facilities. Mills such as Gilfach, Pantybarcud and Esger view were all located along rutted cart-tracks, well away from village settlements. For as long as these rural mills remained in production and some were in production in the late nineteen fifties, they still used the water-driven machinery installed in the mills, when they were first built. For carding they had hand-fed scribblers, for spinning they had hand mules, warping was done on wall pegs and weaving with narrow-width power looms. They produced blankets and carthenni that had to be sewn together to produce double-sized bedcovers and a wide range of products ranging from shirt flannel to rough suitings and from knitting yarn to under-wear flannel.

Of the Dre-fach mills, the following could be regarded as falling within the category of the small rural mill, employing few staff and dependent on out-dated water-driven machinery:

Bargod Mills	Aberbrân	Ogof
Esger View	Glanbargod	Dangribyn
Rhydwern	Cwm Gilfach	Pantybarcud

The second type of mill found in the Dre-fach Felindre district was of the more urban type employing anything up to a hundred workers together with out-workers. Some of them were completely new ventures, built mostly in the eighteen nineties, but some like the Dolwion and Coedmôr mills began as fulling mills. Others like the Cambrian and Dyffryn were rebuilt on the site of earlier weaving shops. Unlike the smaller, older mills, the larger factories were not of necessity located near the source of water power, for good road and rail communications were important. They depended on a wholesale rather than a retail market and the mills were usually run by non-working owners, who in many cases built impressive dwellings near the mills. Many amassed considerable wealth from textile production and many became leaders of the communities in which they lived.

For driving the mill machinery, the owners installed gas producer engines and later electric power to drive the most modern machinery available at the time. In most cases the machinery was bought from Yorkshire manufacturers. Neither were they content with using local wools alone for their products, but fine New Zealand and other imported wools were widely used. Markets too were further away than those of the small rural mills and some had their own retail shops in industrial regions. Dyffryn mills for example did have a retail shop in Middlesbrough and later in Cardiff for the sale of its products.

The Cambrian Mills were typical of the larger type of urban mill built in the Teifi valley between 1890 and 1912. The lease of the land was obtained by David Lewis of Pantglas from William Lewes of Llysnewydd and a large comprehensive mill was built between 1910 and 1912. The mill started as a weaving shop and dwelling

Cambrian Mills in its heyday

house called Doldywyll, and the most modern machinery then available was installed in the new mill building by David Lewis. The mill remained in the possession of the Lewis family; the son of the founder, John Lewis, purchasing the mill from his father in 1912, until 1951 when it was taken over by Messrs. David Evans Bevan Ltd., of Neath. A new owner, the Tra-môr Company, purchased it in 1968. During the Lewis occupation, the Cambrian was a well equipped comprehensive mill employing over 50 people with many out-workers. Most of its machinery dated from just before the first world war and power until about 1960 was supplied by a 150 horse power gas suction plant. Equipment consisted of:

Steam boiler for cloth finishing
Two willeys. One for white, the other for colours

Four 60 inch carding engines each consisting of hopper feed
3 part scribbler, Scotch intermediate feed
2 part carder with 4 height tape condenser giving 100 good
threads each
Six self-acting mules 3 of 250 spindles, 3 of 400 spindles
Sykes ring-twister of 40 spindles
Warp bobbin winder of 50 spindles
120 inch warping mill and creel
Three Universal weft winders of 20 spindles each
Thirty five power looms
    Three 90 inch Dobcross 4 box, 16 shaft
    Three 100 inch single box, 4 shafts
    One 20 inch, single box, 4 shafts
    Three 100 inch single box, 4 shafts
    One 40 inch 4 shafts with revolving box
    Twenty four, 40 inch 2 shafts, single box
Four fulling machines
Drop-hammer scourer
Hydro extractor
Broad-width tenter
Squeeze rollers attached to a tank for carbonizing
Rotary steam press
120 inch Mozer raiser
Rolling and folding machine
Two dye vats

A comprehensive range of flannels, blankets, carthenni and garments was produced at the Cambrian in its heyday. Today the old Cambrian Mill houses the National Woollen Museum, established in 1976. A fully working weaving mill – Melin Teifi – occupies a part of the extensive premises.

The refurbished National Woollen Museum, 2004

Museum Entrance Gallery, 2004

Hot steam boiler

Fulling machine

Wool weighing

Great wheel for spinning

Mozer raiser

Spinning wheels

National Woollen Museum Finishing Shop – Tenter Box

Cutting table at the museum

Finished products

*Different mill patterns
from all over Wales*

A woven carthen *produced in a
number of northern Wales mills
to mark an investiture at Caernarfon
castle in 1911.*

Warp in place on a hand-loom

The museum shop – displaying finished products

National Woollen Museum – entrance

*A variety of woollen products
at the shop*

Flannel night gowns

Cafe and retail shop at the museum entrance

Rolls of cloth at the mill, National Woollen Museum

Fire at the Dyffryn Mills, 1923

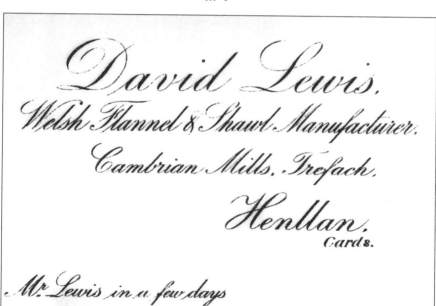

David Lewis of Cambrian's Trade Card

Eclipse

During the first world war, the woollen industry of Dre-fach flourished. Mills were re-organized, new machinery was purchased and extra staff was engaged to meet the overwhelming demand for flannel, blankets and uniform material. The mills flourished on government contracts and anyone who could card, spin or weave took full advantage of the situation. W.P. Crankshaw in 1925, for example[16] describes how one factory owner commenced business by leasing a smallholding, 'containing a building in which were still the willey and carding engine originally used for making carded rolls for hand spinners. He picked up here and there a spinning mule, a couple of hand looms and a milling machine at a total cost of about £26, and was thereby enabled to commence work with a supply of wool obtained on credit'.

Much of the flannel produced during the war was 'angola', an inferior mixture of wool and cotton that was widely used for making army shirts. This was very cheap to produce, but the demand for it was so heavy, that its sale brought much profit to the textile manufacturers of western Wales. In 1915, for example, one small mill alone, the Pantybarcud Mill at Cwmhiraeth, fulfilled a War Office contract for five hundred dozen shirts. The profits accumulated by a few textile manufacturers were invested in buying capital equipment.

A Labourers' Union was formed as early as 1900 in the Teifi valley for in the parishes of Llangeler and Pen-boyr alone at the time there were 260 male weavers and the same number of women and children employed in the woollen industry. The Labourers' Union included all the male and female workers in the two parishes and a few years later the boundaries of the Union were extended to include the Pencader district as well. A piece-rate scale was fixed for the different branches as well as a daily wage scale. The Union continued until the nineteen-twenties.

While War Office contracts continued, profits were high and the industry flourished. But the mills of western Wales were not geared to meet conditions in the highly competitive conditions of

Rhydwern Mill

the post-war era. As one manufacturer lamented, 'Henllan increased its machinery and productive capacity during the war and has not since increased its market; it has merely increased the competition in a market which has the bottom knocked out of it'. It seems likely, however, that if more factories had been re-equipped with the proceeds of war and the standards of workmanship improved, then the industry would have been in a much stronger position to withstand the depressed conditions of the inter-war period.

By 1920, the seeds of depression was already bearing fruit and the period 1920-5, in particular, was one of great difficulty in western Wales. Government surplus stock of flannel and blankets was thrown on the open market at ridiculously low prices, so that the woollen manufacturers were forced to meet this unfair competition by cutting their costs and prices. Flannel shirts, for example, which were sold at 52 shillings and 6 pence a dozen, wholesale, in 1916, were sold at 38 shillings a dozen in 1923. The golden age was over; the price of wool fell from an all time high of

Frondeg Mill, Cwmhiraeth

54 pence in 1919 to as little as 9 pence per pound in 1921 and 7½ pence in 1922. The wages of textile workers were cut and hundreds were dismissed in the losing battle of making ends meet.

To add to all the other difficulties, the southern Wales miners went on strike in April 1921, and since southern Wales was still the main market for the textiles of western Wales, the consequences were very serious indeed.[17] It was made even worse by conditions in the mining valleys after the strike had ended in June 1921. 'Wages were slashed, price lists were cut, privileges were taken away, victimization became rife'.[18] No longer could southern Wales provide the assured market for the products of rural woollen mills. For example, a wholesaler at Merthyr Vale, Glamorgan, bought the following value of goods from Pantybarcud Mill, Dre-fach, between 1914 and 1922. The goods were made up of shirts, flannel, aprons, blankets and 'drovers' (drawers).

1914	£7	7	3½ d.
1915	£10	4	8
1916	£6	19	4
1917	£9	6	9
1918	£11	8	6
1919	£10	4	6
1920	£9	2	6
1921		7	4½
1922	None		

Another wholesaler at Maesteg, Glamorgan, paid £165 12s. 0d. in 1917 but his order had dwindled to £3 4s. 6d. in 1921 and no orders at all were received from him after that date.

The woollen manufacturers of western Wales failed in their attempt to meet changing conditions; many still produced inferior angola as they had done in wartime, but they failed to sell it. Most of them still concentrated on the production of flannel for shirts, vests, and 'drovers', but the demand for underwear flannel fell rapidly in the early nineteen twenties. The introduction of knitted underwear produced by the hosiery manufacturers of the east Midlands, Scotland and the north of England had an enormous effect on the demand for woven woollen goods generally. In the post-war era, knitwear became available in the shops of southern Wales. 'Flannel is now only worn by babies and old people', said a contemporary observer,[19] 'the flannel trade of former times will never come back; it went out with flannel petticoats'. Yet the mills of western Wales still produced thousands of yards of flannel, which they could not sell. Fewer people required the striped-shirting flannel, the linsey skirts, the kersey drawers, and the fringed nursing shawls that were still produced by the textile manufacturers of Dre-fach. A change in fashion meant too that the hard, thick, tweed-suitings produced by the factories were no longer in demand, and as a result many village tailors went out of business. Many of these tailors made a living by making up their customers' own cloth, which had been woven in a local factory. Some were itinerant craftsmen who paid periodic visits to the farms and cottages of the region, making up clothes for the families in their homes. In the nineteen-twenties, more and more of their work was being taken over by specialized outfitters in the towns. Some of them were chain tailoring businesses who were unwilling to make up a customer's cloth.[20] With the arrival of the large outfitters' shops, ready-made suits became increasingly popular and killed the trade in Welsh homespuns and tweeds. Besides the competition of more attractive materials, Welsh flannel was affected by cheaper substitutes such as unions and cotton flannelette, which could be obtained from local shops or through mail order stores. Mail order businesses, Messrs. J. D. Williams and Messrs. Oxendale of Manchester in particular, were gaining in popularity in the early twenties and the ease of ordering cheap textiles from their warehouses had a very harmful effect on the sale of locally-produced woollen goods.

It is unfortunate that the textile manufacturers of western Wales were unable to meet the challenge of changing circumstances. It was beyond their ability to produce the lighter, more fashionable fabrics that the public demanded. As a result, many of the factories were forced to close down.[21]

Undoubtedly, the main reason why the western Wales woollen industry declined was the inability of the manufacturers to introduce new fabrics and new methods of production. 'Whilst I have frequently expressed my admiration of these fine old craftsmen', says Crankshaw, 'it should be said that their skill as workers is somewhat discounted by their strict adherence to traditional methods and fabrics. They generally fail to achieve excellence through inability to break from these traditional ideas and to adapt themselves to modern circumstances and materials'.

Many of the mills of western Wales, even during the period of war-time prosperity, were run as part-time businesses in conjunction with agriculture. In many cases, the farm was the main interest of the mill-owner and the machinery in his mill was often entirely neglected for long periods when other occupations demanded attention. As a rule the mill and farm were run as joint enterprises and as long as they yielded a living between them, the farmer-woollen manufacturer was perfectly happy. In many cases, the holdings run by mill-owners were small and did not interfere

Dyffryn Mills

with the running of the mill. In other cases textile manufacturing was secondary to farming pursuits. Crankshaw, during his survey in 1925, saw mills that accommodated butter churns, cheese presses, and even cattle. In one case, 'the farmer-manufacturer who appeared with a scythe on his shoulder . . . begged us to come again another day, "as I have two men in the field and cannot leave them".'[22] Workers were often engaged to help with farm work as well as textile manufacturing and this in itself did not contribute to a high degree of skill in employees.

Many of the small mills were run on most unbusiness-like methods; accounts were kept to a minimum, even if they were kept at all. 'Books are not necessary,' said one manufacturer, 'we can trust our customers'. Those that surveyed the industry in the nineteen-twenties and even in the nineteen-forties found it impossible to ascertain the cost of production. 'Cost of production appears to be unknown', says Crankshaw. 'Selling prices are fixed in a most arbitrary manner, usually in comparison with the prices ruling in the market or in the fair, without any apparent reference to actual cost and possible difference in quality. "Selling price is the best price available," said one. Another takes wholesale orders for flannel at 6d. per yard less than his retail price, without having any idea whether the transaction is profitable.'[23]

In many of the mills of western Wales in the nineteen-twenties, the approach was, to say the least, lackadaisical. Neither men nor machinery were employed in the most economical manner. Most of the weavers were middle aged, for the industry was failing to attract young people, and many of the weavers were not prepared to change their methods of working nor were they prepared to undergo a period of training. Many of the weavers had been trained on hand looms, and when power looms were introduced into the industry generally they could not imagine the

Meiros Mills

possibility of one man being able to look after more than one loom. 'It was not uncommon', noted Crankshaw, 'to find a fully trained weaver looking after a loom, running at a very moderate speed, whereas in Yorkshire and the other textile manufacturing districts it was common practice for one person, often a woman, to look after a pair of double-width power-looms'.

Not only was machinery not put to the best use, but in many cases machinery was liable to break down at frequent intervals. There were no competent textile engineers in the region who were capable of repairing the machines. Thus in the mills of western Wales, one found not only a great deal of obsolete machinery but also a great deal that had been roughly repaired and very liable to break down again. Often the breakage of a piece of machinery meant weeks of waiting before a local blacksmith, carpenter or handyman could undertake repair work. Woollen manufacturers were also liable to buy second-hand machinery in Yorkshire, rather than spend a little more on the newest type of machine. Although some of the larger factories were re-equipped with new machinery between 1910 and 1922, far too many mill owners were content to use the machinery that had been installed when the mills were built, possibly forty years before. Even the machinery installed at that time could have been second-hand. Others combed Yorkshire and the west of England for the bargain rejects of the mills of those regions. 'It almost appears', says Crankshaw,[24] 'that when the knowledge of the introduction of spinning machinery reached the Welsh manufacturer, which seems to have been about fifty years after it had taken place in other woollen manufacturing districts, he proceeded to bring himself up to date by purchasing what those other centres were casting aside as useless'. Hand mules of mid-nineteenth century date were still being bought by some woollen manufacturers in the Teifi valley in 1914 and 1916, and power looms that had already done thirty or forty years' service in Yorkshire mills were still in constant demand in the mills of Drefach. But even worse than using antiquated looms and mules was the general condition of the carding engines. This had a disastrous effect on the quality of cloth, for efficient carding is the key to the quality of yarn. Without good yarn, no loom, however modern it may be, can produce cloth of high quality. 'The very sight of some of the carding engines is enough to drive any well trained carder to commit suicide. Almost without exception . . . carding engines require re-clothing . . . If only this could be done, the position would not be so hopeless'.[25]

Another great difficulty facing the rural woollen manufacturer was that in many cases the mill building and even the plant and machinery were owned by an absentee landlord. One mill, the Glanesger in Dre-fach, for example, was owned by a Harley Street medical practitioner and was rented on a forty-year lease from 1904. The machinery and building of the Glanesger mill, in common with many others, were under the control of an absentee landlord, and tenants of mills of this type were in a hopeless position for they had to beg even for essential repairs. The renewal of machinery was out of the question. There was no incentive for the tenant to spend money on improvements, knowing that the period of lease was limited and that in many cases both machinery and building reverted to the landlord on the expiration of the term.

As a result of all these complex factors, the woollen industry of western Wales declined very rapidly in the nineteen-twenties.[26] General untidiness and wasteful methods, due to lack of supervision and inadequate training of workers, was apparent everywhere. The true atmosphere of a textile manufacturing district, as one would find in the towns of the West Riding of Yorkshire and the west of England was completely absent from western Wales, for even at its most flourishing the woollen industry was very much secondary to farming and the influence of farming interests and outlook may have accounted for the unbusinesslike methods of running mills.

Many of the mills struggled on, but the golden age had passed never to return again. From 1922 to 1939 the story of the industry was one of contraction and the mills had to look for much wider markets than the mining valleys of southern Wales. More and more goods were being sold to wholesale drapers in Birmingham, London, Manchester and other cities. Considerably less was sold to drapers in such places as Pontypridd, Merthyr and Maesteg, while

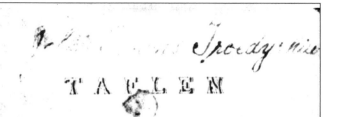

TAFLEN

BRISIAU

GWEHYDDION

VELINDRE, DREFACH,

A'R CYLCHOEDD.

Newcastle-Emlyn:

PRINTED BY JOHN RICHARD DAVIES,

1891.

Weavers' price list

No.		d.
1	Stripe Panedig ... ... per yard	3¾
2	¾yd. Working Shirts; black & white ...	4
3	⅞ „ „ „	4½
4	¾ Peisiau bach Stripe	3½
5	⅞ „ „	3¾
6	¾ Crysau llwyd plod	4½
7	„ „ stripe	3¾
8	⅞ „ plod	5
9	„ „ stripe	4¼
10	1yd. „ plod	5½
11	1yd. „ stripe	4¾
12	¾ Crysau coch, 'dafedd yn stofi, plod ...	4½
13	„ „ worsted, „ plod ...	5½
14	„ Crysau dau-las plod	4½
15	„ „ stripe...	3¾
16	⅞ & ¾ Ffedogau bach plod	4½
17	„ „ „ stripe	3¾
18	„ „ Billy Ffwdan plod	6½
19	„ „ stripe	4¼
20	„ „ with border, stripe ...	4¾
21	¾ Cwlwm Cariad a 'dafedd	6
22	„ „ cotton a gwlan, neu worsted	6½
23	„ „ worsted i gyd	7½
24	⅞ & ¾ Ffedogau dau-las plod	4½
25	„ „ „ stripe	3¾
26	1yd. „ plod	5
27	„ „ dau-las stripe	4¼
28	¾ Peisiau dau-las stripe	3¾
29	⅞ „ „	4¼
30	Peisiau cross	5
31	„ „ with chains	5½
32	¾ Come Boys	5½
33	„ Peisiau cotton fine, plain	5½
34	„ „ chains...	6
35	⅞ „ plain	6
36	„ „ with chains	6½
37	1yd. „ plain	6½
38	„ „ with chains	7
39	⅞ Peisiau, worsted yn stofi (chains) ...	7
40	1yd. „ „ „	7½
41	¾ Worsted du, 'dafedd yn gwau	4¾
42	„ „ lliwiau yn croesi	5½
43	„ „ 'dafedd yn gwau (chains) ...	6
44	1yd. „ plain	6¼
45	„ „ lliwiau yn croesi	7
46	„ „ with chains	7½
47	1¼ „ plain	7
48	Worsted du, lliwiau yn croesi ... per yard	8
49	„ „ with chains	8½
50	¾ Cotton du, plain	5¼
51	„ „ chains	6½
52	1yd. „ plain	7¼
53	„ „ lliwiau yn croesi	8
54	„ „ chains	8½
55	1¼ „ plain	7¾
56	„ „ lliwiau yn croesi	8½
57	„ „ chains	9
58	¾ Stwff coch (worsted No. 24.)	4¾
59	„ „ („ No. 30.)	5¾
60	„ Plain Poplin	6¼
61	„ Serge, 'dafedd yn gwau	6¾
62	„ „ worsted „	7¼
63	Rob Roy, plod	5½
64	„ stripe	4¾
65	¾ Plod coch, 'dafedd yn stofi	4½
66	„ „ „ stripe... ...	3¾
67	„ Bwmbast a gwlan, plod	4¾
68	„ „ stripe	4¼
69	„ „ Kersey plod	6½
70	⅞ & ¾ Gwlanen fach, coch a glas, plod ...	4½
71	„ „ „ „ stripe ...	3¼
72	¾ Camrhedynen	6
73	„ Gwlanen Wen	3¾
74	⅞ „	4
75	1yd. „	4½
76	¾ Serge 'dafedd	5¼
77	1¼ Blankedi plain (arferol)	3½
78	1½ „ „	4
79	1¼ Blankedi Kersey	4¾
80	1yd. Sheets „	5¼
81	1¼ „ „	6
82	¾ Brethyn Cordeddog, plod	4½
83	„ „ single „	5
84	1yd. Kersey Cloth „	6½
85	„ „ stripe	5¾
86	„ 'Dafedd dwbl, Camrhedynen, plod ...	6
87	„ „ „ stripe ...	5¼
88	„ Brethin Plain, plod	5
89	„ „ stripe	4¼
90	„ „ Chains 2's, gwau 1 a 1 single ...	7½
91	„ „ „ „ 1 a 1 dwbl ...	6
92	1½ Brethin Plain	4¾
93	1¼ „ Kersey, stripe	6¾
94	¾ Kersey Dr'overs ... ... per yard	4¾
95	1yd. Ffedogau â border plod a stripe ...	5½
96	1½ „ „ ...	6½
97	¾ Large plod, Badger	6½
98	„ Small „	7
99	„ Minco, tair plaid	6¼
100	„ Camrhedynen, worsted i gyd	8¼
101	„ „ 'dafedd yn gwau	7¼
102	Crysau Steel Grey, plod, lledi'r Meiros ...	4¾
103	1yd. Turnovers, plod & stripe... ... each	9
104	1¼ „ „ ... ... each	10½
105	2yd. Shawls, „ ... ... each	3s.
106		
107		
108		
109		
110		
111		
112		
113		
114		
115		
116		
117		
118	Stofi 20 yards	6d.
119	„ „ Shawls	1s.

N.B—Special Prices for Special Pieces. Prices to be decided by a Committee of four, two Masters and two Workmen, viz. :—

Masters {SAMUEL WILLIAMS, Dyffryn Mills. / DANIEL LEWIS, Frondeg Mills.

Workmen {EBENEZER EVANS, Perthiteg. / THOMAS WILLIAMS, Pontbren.

STANDARD WIDTHS :—¾. ⅞. 1. 1¼. 1½. 1¾ yards. Any intermediate widths for the price of the nearest standard, and if it happens to be exactly in the middle between two standards, for the price of the next lower. Widths of Flannels to be measured when scoured and finished.

STANDARD LENGTHS :—

Every Piece Warped up to 20 yards, to be paid 21 yards.
„ „ 30 „ „ 32 „
„ „ 40 „ „ 43 „
„ „ 50 & 51 „ 54 & 55 [respectively.
„ „ 60 & 63 „ 65 & 68 [ditto.

Dated January 9th, 1891.

direct sales to local farmers dwindled almost to nothing. There was also a change in the character of goods manufactured. Before 1925 a large part of the production was concerned with the manufacture of shirt and underwear flannel, knitting wools and heavy tweeds. After that date, mills began to concentrate on blankets and patterned bedcovers. By 1935, the tourist trade of western Wales had increased to such an extent that direct selling to the public from the mills became increasingly important. Woollen mills became tourist attractions and some flourished on the proceeds of sales to the holidaying public. Nevertheless the thirties were not a flourishing period for the textile manufacturers; the industry contracted as more and more mills were closed.[27] There was a revival during the 1939-45 war, so that in 1947, the following were in full production in the Dre-fach Felindre district:

Dyffryn	Alltcafan
Glanbargod	Coedmôr
Rhydwern	Glanesger
Derw	Pantybarcud
Esger View	Square Hall
Dôl-goch	Dolwion
Cambrian	Bargod Mills

Since 1947 the position in the woollen industry of western Wales has worsened steadily, for although the markets for textile products has been extended considerably, particularly with the introduction of double-weave (tapestry) bedcovers, furnishing fabrics and lighter tweeds, the number of mills supplying the market has declined greatly. It may seem surprising that many well-placed, modernized and efficient mills like Square Hall have been forced to go out of business. The main reason for the contraction of the industry has been the difficulty experienced by mill-owners in recruiting suitable labour. Every factory in the region employs less labour than it did in 1947. It has been well-nigh impossible to find trained labour, mainly because wages in the textile industry compare very unfavourable with those paid in other occupations. Indeed throughout the post-war period the basic wage paid to textile workers had been constantly well below the wage paid to agricultural labourers. Consequently farming and work in various government establishments in western Wales claimed labour at the expense of the woollen mills.

But not only have mill-owners been unable to recruit an appreciable labour force, but there have also been great difficulties in finding well-trained people to act as foremen and managers. When textile manufacturers have wished to retire from business it has been extremely difficult to find someone to buy factories.[28] Consequently many mills have gone out of business for this reason alone.

In 2004 two working mills – Dolwerdd at Cwmpengraig and Melin Teifi in the old Cambrian Mills are in production and no longer can Dre-fach Felindre be regarded as a scene of great industrial activity. No longer is the village 'The Huddersfield of Wales'.

The National Woollen Museum, a branch of the National Museums and Galleries of Wales, sets out to trace the history of the most widespread of Welsh industries in the most imortant region. Opened in 1976, the museum was completely refurbished as a result of a Lottery grant and it was reopened to the public in 2004.

Footnotes

[1] Jones, Daniel E.: *Hanes Plwyfi Llangeler a Phenboyr* (Llandysul, 1899), p. 357.

[2] Noyadd Trefawr MSS 154 (National Library of Wales).

[3] Jones, *op. cit.*, p. 357.

[4] Maudet Penhouet. B.L.: *Letters describing a Tour through a part of South Wales by a Pedestrian Traveller* (1797), p. 86.

[5] Roy Evans Deeds 98 (National Library of Wales).

[6] Noyadd Deeds 154 (National Library of Wales).

[7] Daniel Jones, *op. cit.*, p. 360, notes the existence of the following weaving factories in 1899: Doldywyll, Central House, Felinfach, Spring Garden, Ogof, Cwmpengraig, Ty'r Lôn, Gilwen Hill, Parc Cerrig, Pensingrug, Siop Pensarn, Llainffald, Bachygwyddyl, Tŷ Newydd, Man-lle-gwaun, Penwalk, Penlon, Glanrhyd, Nantybargod.

[8] Account book 65.254, Welsh Folk Museum Archives.

[9] Transcript of conversation (translation) with the late Mrs M. Jones in July, 1965.

[10] Jones, *op. cit.*, p. 360.

[11] Ibid, p. 361.

[12] Taflen Brisiau 1891 ed.

[13] Jones, *op. cit.*, p. 361.

[14] *Ibid.*, p. 362.

[15] *Ibid.*, p. 362.

[16] I am grateful to the late Mr William Davies, Durham, for this verse.

[17] Jones, *op. cit.*, p. 361.

[18] Crankshaw, W. P.: Report on a Survey of the Welsh Textile Industry made on behalf of the University of Wales (Cardiff, 1927), p. 18.

[19] *Ibid.*, p. 9.

[20] *Ibid.*, p. 15.

[21] Lewis, E. D.: *The Rhonda Valleys* (Cardiff, 1959), p. 250.

[22] Crankshaw, *op. cit.*, p. 15.

[23] Well-known shops that were established in the 1920s in such towns as Hwlffordd (*Haverfordwest*), Abergwaun (*Fishguard*), Aberteifi (*Cardigan*), Aberystwyth and Caerfyrddin (*Carmarthen*) were Messrs. Burton, Hepworth and Hodges

[24] Crankshaw, *op. cit.*, p. 15.

[25] *Ibid.*, p. 15.

[26] *Ibid.*; and Jones, A. M.: *The Welsh Woollen Industry*, University of Wales, M.Sc. thesis (1925) (unpublished).

[27] Rural Industries Bureau, *Survey of the Welsh Woollen Industry* (unpublished 1947) and Evans, G., *The Welsh Woollen Indsutry, Recent History and Present Position* (unpublished University of Wales M.A. thesis, 1948).

[28] Glenesger Mill closed in 1944 because the owner would not grant a renewal of lease.